HOW TO SURVIVE IN THE DESERT

Ruth Owen

Skull, Namibia

Publisher: *Melissa Fairley*
Art Director: *Faith Booker*
Editor: *Emma Dods*
Designer: *Emma Randall*
Production Controller: *Ed Green*
Production Manager: *Suzy Kelly*

ISBN: 978 1 84898 213 0

Picture credits (t=top; b=bottom; c=centre; l=left; r=right; OFC=outside front cover; OBC=outside back cover):
John Cancalosi/ardea.com: 13t. Michael Freeman/Corbis: 7. George Grall/Getty Images: 24. imagebroker/Alamy: 28–29.
iStock: OFCc, OBCb. Mauritius/SuperStock: 26. Shutterstock: OFCbl, OFCt, 1, 2, 4, 5, 6 (both), 8 (both), 9t, 10,
11 (both), 12t, 16 (all), 17 (both), 18-19 (all), 20–21 (all), 22–23, 25, 27 (both), 29t (both), 31C, 31D, OBCt.
Karl Terblanche/ardea.com: 12b. Anne-Marie Weber/Corbis: 9b, 31A. Woods Wheatcroft/Getty Images: 14, 31B.
Gordon Wiltsie/Getty Images: 13b. www.janespencer.com: 15.

Thank you to Lorraine Petersen and the members of *nasen*.

Every effort has been made to trace copyright holders, and we apologize in advance for any omissions.
We would be pleased to insert the appropriate acknowledgements in any subsequent edition of this publication.

NOTE TO READERS
The website addresses are correct at the time of publishing. However, due to the ever-changing
nature of the Internet, websites and content may change. Some websites can contain links that
are unsuitable for children. The publisher is not responsible for changes in content or website
addresses. We advise that Internet searches should be supervised by an adult.

Neither the publishers nor the author shall be liable for any bodily harm or damage to property whatsoever
that may be caused or sustained as a result of conducting any of the activities featured in this book.

*Sahara Desert,
North Africa*

CONTENTS

CHAPTER 1

LOST IN THE DESERT

In your everyday life you have everything you need to survive.

**Turn on the tap and water pours out.
Pick up the phone and a pizza is on its way!**

But what would happen if one day all that changed?

What would happen if you were driving across
a desert and your car broke down?

Would you know how to survive...

...in a desert?

Canyon

A desert can also have huge sand dunes.

Dunes

There are often sandstorms in sandy deserts.

Sandstorm

How to survive a sandstorm:
- If you cannot get to shelter, lie or sit down.
- Close your eyes or put on glasses.
- Cover your nose and mouth with some cloth.
- Point your body in the direction you were walking.

After the storm, everything will be covered in sand.
Everything will look different and you might get lost.

In a desert, everything looks the same. Look out for landmarks, such as a bush or a large rock.

Landmark

In the dry desert air, things can seem closer than they actually are. Always multiply your estimated distance by three – that's a desert survival trick!

If you are in a broken-down car, stay at the site if you can.

You may have to leave the site to find water and food. If this happens, make a large arrow to show rescuers which direction you took.

Rescue dog

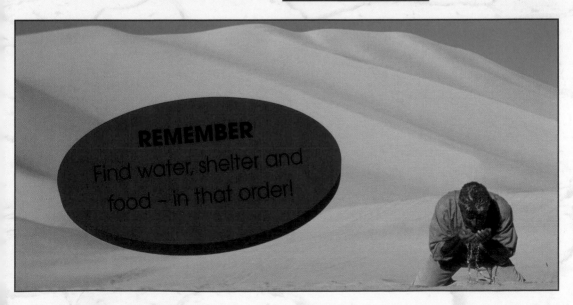

REMEMBER
Find water, shelter and food – in that order!

CHAPTER 2

FINDING WATER

In a hot desert, lack of water is your biggest enemy.

Your body cools off by sweating. The more you sweat, the more water your body loses.

If your body does not have enough water to sweat, you will get heatstroke. Heatstroke will make you pass out.

Find shade.

Do not take off your clothes. Cover your head and neck, too. Your clothes will soak up your sweat. The wet clothes will keep your body cool.

In a hot desert, your body needs one litre of water every hour. Sip water as often as you can.

Your wee should be pale yellow. If your wee is dark yellow, you are not getting enough water.

Tips on how to find water in the desert...

Storm clouds gather

Keep watch for storm clouds. Use anything you have to catch rainwater.

Dune ant

Look out for ants. A long line of ants on a tree could be visiting some trapped water.

Birds need water, too. Look for bird droppings on rocks. There might be water in a rock crack nearby.

Gambel's quail

If you find a dried-up stream, dig a hole. There could be water underground.

Dried-up stream

CHAPTER 3

SHELTER

If you do not already have a shelter, you will need to find or build one. In a desert, the daytime temperature can be 60°C.

The shelter will give you shade. This will keep you cool during the day. It will help your body to use less water.

Cave

If you have a blanket or sheet of plastic, you can build an underground shelter.

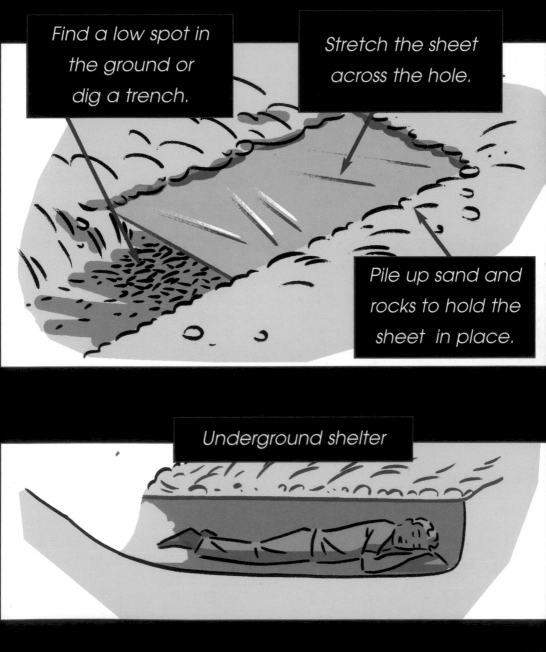

Find a low spot in the ground or dig a trench.

Stretch the sheet across the hole.

Pile up sand and rocks to hold the sheet in place.

Underground shelter

CHAPTER 4

FIRE

If you can find material to burn, build a fire. A fire can be used for cooking and will keep you warm at night.

To build a fire you need tinder, kindling and fuel.

First light the tinder.

Use dry grass for tinder.

Then you help the fire to burn using the kindling.

Use dry leaves or small twigs for kindling.

Use dry wood or dry animal dung for fuel.

Finally, you add fuel to make the fire burn for a long time.

If you have no matches, you will need to improvise. This means finding a new way to do something. A lens from glasses or a camera will catch sunlight. Direct the sunlight onto the tinder. It will get hot and catch fire.

Lens

CHAPTER 5

FINDING FOOD

In a desert, it is more important to find water than food. A healthy person can go for about 60 days without food.

Your body uses up water digesting food.
So, if you only have a little water, don't eat.

You can eat insects such as ants, termites, beetles and grasshoppers. You can also eat insect larvae.

Ants

Beetle

Termite hill

Grasshopper

Insect larva

19

The baobab tree grows in deserts in Africa and Australia. You can boil young baobab leaves in water to make soup.

You can eat the tree's fruits. Eat the soft pulp and seeds.

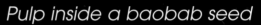
Pulp inside a baobab seed

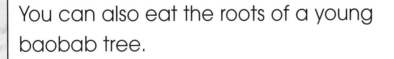
Baobab tree

You can also eat the roots of a young baobab tree.

There are lots of snakes in the desert.
You might have to kill one to protect yourself.

Don't waste the meat! The snake's venom
is behind its head. So, cut the snake in
half. Then cook and eat the tail end.

Spitting cobra

If you don't have a knife, you will need to look for
an animal skeleton. A sharp piece of smashed
bone can be used as a knife.

CHAPTER 6

DESERT DANGERS

In the desert, there are many creatures that bite or sting.

In a survival situation you may have no medicine. So, remember these rules to stay safe:

- Never put your hands or bare feet somewhere that you cannot see.
- Check your shoes before you put them on.
- Shake out your clothes before you put them on.
- Carefully check the ground before sitting or lying down.

Scorpions are relatives of spiders. They have a venomous sting on their tails.

Scorpion in the desert

The Mojave rattlesnake lives in deserts in North America.

Its venom stops your nerves carrying messages to your muscles. This means you cannot breathe.

You will die within hours of being bitten if you don't get treatment.

Mojave rattlesnake

The Gila monster lives in deserts
in the United States and Mexico.

It is a type of lizard that can
grow up to 50 centimetres long.

Gila monster

If you get too close, the Gila monster might bite.
It uses its sharp teeth to hold on tight. Venom from
its lower jaw will enter the wound.

CHAPTER 7

PROTECT YOUR BODY

You must keep your body clean in a survival situation. Dirty skin can become infected and cause illness.

If you do not have much water, take an "air bath".

Take off all your clothes before the day gets hot. Expose your body to the air for one hour.

Arak tree

In ancient times, people in the desert used twigs to clean their teeth. The twigs came from the Arak tree.

If you get sunburn, find an aloe vera plant. Cut open a leaf. Spread the plant's juice on your sunburn.

Leaf

Aloe vera

Aloe vera juice

CHAPTER 8

RESCUE

You need to make sure a rescue plane can see you.

Making a fire is a good way to get noticed.

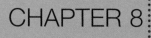

You can send messages to a rescue plane, too. Use rocks to make these signs. Pilots around the world know what they mean.

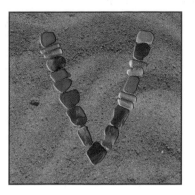 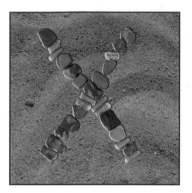

V means "help is needed".
X means "medical help is needed".

If a plane sees your signs, it will rock its wings from side to side.

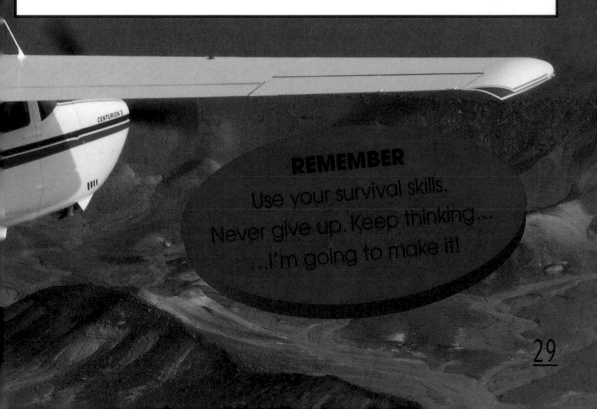

REMEMBER
Use your survival skills.
Never give up. Keep thinking…
…I'm going to make it!

NEED TO KNOW WORDS

canyon A valley with steep cliff-like walls. A canyon is cut into the earth by flowing water. It can take thousands or millions of years to form.

desert A dry area where less than 15 centimetres of rain falls each year.

dew Water that forms when water vapour in the air cools down and turns into water. Dew normally forms at night.

dune A hill made from sand. A dune forms when the wind blows large quantities of sand into a pile that gets bigger and bigger.

heatstroke A condition that can happen when the body gets too hot and cannot cool itself. A person with heatstroke will feel ill and dizzy. They may pass out. If the condition gets worse, it can harm the brain, liver, kidneys and other parts of the body.

landmark Something that a person can use to work out where they are.

larva A young of many insects, including ants and termites. Larvae hatch from eggs. They are also called grubs.

pulp The soft part of a fruit inside the skin or shell.

termite A small insect that looks similar to an ant. Termites live in large colonies.

venom A poison that is deliberately passed onto a victim through a bite or sting.

venomous Describes an animal that uses venom to kill its prey (the animals it eats) or to defend itself.

water vapour A mass of tiny water droplets that look like mist.

SURVIVAL PATTERNS

In a survival situation you must form a survival pattern.

The pattern will put your daily tasks in order – the most important first.

You must stick to your pattern each day.

Here are the things that will be in a desert survival pattern:

Water

Shelter

Fire

Food

SURVIVAL ONLINE

Desert survival tips
www.discoverychannel.co.uk/survival_zone/environments/desert/
index.shtml

Facts and pictures of desert life around the world
http://environment.nationalgeographic.com/environment/habitats/
desert-profile.html

Find out how to build a special pit for collecting water, called a "still".
www.desertusa.com/mag98/dec/stories/water.html

INDEX